Contents

Off to Mexico!

We are going to Mexico. I am very excited because there is so much to see.

We are going to travel all over the country. The places we are visiting are marked on the map.

UNITED STATES OF AMERICA

Chihuahua

Sierra Madre Occidental

Sierra Madre Oriental

Rio Bravo

Los Mochis

Monterrey

Gulf of Mexico

Cancun

Chichen Itza

YUCATAN PENINSULA

Caribbean Sea

Guadalajara

Mexico City

Veracruz

Palenque

BELIZE

Pacific Ocean

M E X I C O

GUATEMALA

HONDURAS

500 kilometres

500 miles

Been There!
MEXICO

Annabel Savery

FRANKLIN
LONDON

Facts about Mexico

Population: 107 million

Capital city: Mexico City

Currency: Peso ($)

Main language: Spanish

Rivers: Bravo, Pánuco, Balsas, Grijalva

Area: 1,964,375 square kilometres (758,449 square miles)

 An Appleseed Editions book

Paperback edition 2014

First published in 2011 by Franklin Watts
338 Euston Road, London NW1 3BH

Franklin Watts Australia
Level 17/207 Kent St, Sydney, NSW 2000

© 2011 Appleseed Editions

Created by Appleseed Editions Ltd,
Well House, Friars Hill, Guestling, East Sussex TN35 4ET

Planning and production by Discovery Books Limited
www.discoverybooks.net
Designed by Ian Winton
Edited by Annabel Savery
Map artwork by Stefan Chabluk
Picture research by Tom Humphrey

ISBN 978 1 4451 3290 7

Dewey Classification: 972'.0842

A CIP catalogue for this book is available from the British Library.

Picture Credits: Alamy Images: p14 (Bruce Coleman Inc.); Corbis: p5 (Danny Lehman), p7 top (Peter Adams), p8 top (Robert Holmes), p12 (Diego Giudice), p13 (Alan Copson), p15 (Craig Lovell), pp18-19 (Franz-Marc Frei), p24 (Frans Lemmens), p26 (Danny Lehman), p27 bottom (Keith Dannemiller), p28 bottom (Danny Lehman), p29 (Jeremy Woodhouse/Blend Images); Galen R Frysinger: p21; Getty Images: p6 (AFP), pp8-9 (Jeremy Woodhouse), pp10-11 (Phil Schermeiseter), p17 (Barcroft Media), p25 (Maria Stenzel), p27 top (Latin Content); Istockphoto: title page & p22 (tompozzo), p16 (PacoRomero), p23 & p31 (ranplett); Shutterstock: p2 (R Gino Santa Maria), p7 middle (Colman Lerner Gerardo), p28 top (ampFotoStudio); Wikimedia: p20 (Daniel Schwen).

Cover photos: Istockphoto: right (PacoRomero); Shutterstock: main (Jiri Vatka), left (Ales Liska).

Printed in Singapore.

Franklin Watts is a division of Hachette Children's Books, an Hachette UK company.
www.hachette.co.uk

In the centre of Mexico is a wide **plateau** and on either side are long mountain ranges called the *Sierra Madre Oriental* and the *Sierra Madre Occidental*. *Sierra Madre* means 'mother range', and *oriental* and *occidental* mean 'eastward' and 'westward'.

Here are some things I know about Mexico...

- Mexico is in the continent of North America. It is a large country, about three times the size of France.

- People wear *sombreros* (right) as part of the national costume. These are big hats with a wide brim to keep off the sun.

- Mexican food is often spicy. Mexican dishes are popular in many countries around the world.

On our trip I'm going to find out lots more!

Arriving in Mexico City

We fly into Mexico City airport in the afternoon. The flight was long and tiring, so we go straight to the hotel in a taxi.

All the taxis look the same. They are all green and white. And they're the same make of car, too.

It takes a long time to travel through the traffic in the city. It is smelly with exhaust fumes. Mexico City is very **polluted**.

Our driver is very friendly and points out special sites as we pass them.

There is a mix of old and new buildings, such as high new hotels and old churches.

Mexico City is the most populous in the world. This means it has more people than any other city. Over nineteen million people live here.

Exploring the capital

The next morning we go into the city centre for breakfast. I have *huevos rancheros*. This is a popular dish in Mexico. There are *tortillas* with fried eggs on top and tasty *salsa*.

Tortillas are made of corn flour and are thin and round like pancakes. They are a common food in Mexico and are eaten in many different ways.

After breakfast we go to the main square in the centre of the city. This is called the *Zocalo*. Around the square are big buildings and in the middle is a huge Mexican flag.

In the city there are big, colourful bullfighting posters. Bullfighting is an old sport that was brought to Mexico by Spanish people.

The Copper Canyon

Today we are at the west-coast port of Los Mochis. From here we will take the train to Chihuahua. On the way we pass through the Copper Canyon. This is part of the Sierra Madre Occidental.

The canyons were made a long time ago by volcanoes. Over time, the sides have been worn away by rivers and rain. Now there are lots of green plants growing on the rocks.

From the train we can see deep into the valley. The journey takes 14 hours. On the way we travel through 86 tunnels and over 37 bridges!

Finally we arrive in the city of Chihuahua. This is the capital of the state of Chihuahua, which is the biggest state in Mexico.

Mountainous Monterrey

From Chihuahua we fly south-east to Monterrey. This is the third largest city in Mexico and the capital of the state of Nuevo Léon. All around the city are the mountains of the Sierra Madre Oriental.

Monterrey is close to the border with the USA. Lots of people from Mexico cross the border illegally to look for better jobs. They send the money they earn home to their families in Mexico.

Mexico and the USA are divided by a big river. This runs a long way along the border, from the state of Chihuahua to the east coast. You can check this on the map on page four.

In Mexico the river is called the Rio Bravo and in the USA the Rio Grande. 'Rio' comes from the Spanish word for river.

South to Veracruz

From Monterrey we travel south down the coast to Veracruz. This is a state on the east coast of Mexico. It is between the mountains and the sea.

The climate here is warm and tropical. Bananas and other foods grow well here. Some foods are grown to be sold in Mexico. Others are **exported**. Selling food to other countries helps to bring money into Mexico.

Each year there are lots of festivals in Mexico. On the train a lady tells us that one of the biggest is the *Dia de Muertos*, or 'Day of the Dead', held on 2 November.

On this day people remember those who have died by dressing-up and making special foods. They visit relatives' graves and set up altars for them. They decorate these with photos and favourite foods.

The Yucatan Peninsula

From Veracruz we fly to the Yucatan **Peninsula**. This is a large piece of land that stretches out into the sea.

A long time ago, people called the Maya had a great civilization in Central America. Some people living in Mexico today are their descendants. The Maya lived mainly on the Yucatan Peninsula. I took this photo of a girl dressed in traditional Mayan clothes.

To the north of the peninsula is the Gulf of Mexico. To the east is the Caribbean Sea.

The land of the Yucatan Peninsula doesn't stop at the coast. It carries on under water like a big shelf. As the water is shallow here it is warm. This makes it a good home for sea creatures, such as lobsters, crabs and fish.

Two Cancuns

Cancun is a big city on the eastern tip of the Yucatan Peninsula. There are two main parts: *Ciudad Cancun* and *Isla Cancun*. We are staying at Isla Cancun.

Isla Cancun is a thin strip of land around a big lagoon.

The beach is long, with white sand and blue sea. I can see why lots of people want to come here. It is very beautiful. But with so many people it is very crowded.

Until about 50 years ago Isla Cancun was home to just a few fishermen and their families. Then the government decided to turn it into a **resort**. Many hotels were built for tourists to stay in.

All the people working on the hotels lived in a small town. This town grew and grew to become the big city of Ciudad Cancun.

Ancient ruins

Today we are going to see some of the ancient buildings that the Maya built. The site is called *Chichen Itza* and it is very famous. We hire a car and drive there from Cancun.

El Castillo

Chichen Itza was a great city of the Mayan people. The biggest building is the *El Castillo* pyramid. There are lots of steep steps up each side. The square part on the top is a temple.

Some of these buildings were built 1,500 years ago and different groups of people have added to them over the centuries. **Archaeologists** study these buildings to find out about these ancient civilizations.

Although Mayan people still live on the Yucatan Peninsula today, many are leaving their traditional farming jobs to look for work in the cities.

In the rainforest

We leave the Yucatan Peninsula and drive south to the city of Palenque. This is another Mayan city. It is in the south of Mexico in the state of Chiapas.

At the city of Palenque we look at the ruins. There are 500 buildings here, but some have not been uncovered for people to look at.

There are many **indigenous** groups living in Chiapas. Most are related to the Mayan people. Different groups speak different languages, but most people understand Spanish too.

The ancient city is in the Palenque National Park. The park also contains the *Selva Lacandona* or Lacandón rainforest. Wild animals such as monkeys, red macaws, toucans and jaguars live here.

Farming in Mexico

From Palenque we have a long car journey to Guadalajara. This part of the trip will take us through lots of countryside.

We will stop at small towns along the way. Here, people wear clothes made from traditional cloth that is made in the region.

Only a quarter of Mexican people live in the countryside; most people live in **urban** areas.

As we travel we see crops growing and people farming. Some people grow food just to feed themselves and their families. This is called **subsistence** farming.

Other farms are bigger and crops are grown to sell to people at markets and in shops. These big farms are called *ejidos*.

Maize

The main crop grown in Mexico is maize. Maize flour (or corn flour) is used to make the tortillas that people eat with most meals.

In Guadalajara city

Guadalajara is the second largest city in Mexico. The city is warm and there are lots of people shopping and talking with friends.

After being in the countryside it is strange being in the city again. Here, many people wear western clothes, such as jeans and t-shirts.

Lots of people in Guadalajara are wearing football shirts. *Fútbol*, or football, is the most popular sport in Mexico. Guadalajara are in the premier division of the Mexican football league.

Children in Mexico have to go to school from the ages of six to fourteen. Different age groups have lessons at different times. Some children start early in the morning and finish at lunchtime. Others start after lunch and go on until the early evening.

Spanish settlers

Exploring Guadalajara is hungry work, so we buy *tacos* from a street stall. These are crunchy tortillas that are folded around beans, cheese and spicy tomato salsa. Yum!

Next, we go to the cathedral. This was built by Spanish people who came to Mexico over 500 years ago. They brought the Roman Catholic religion with them.

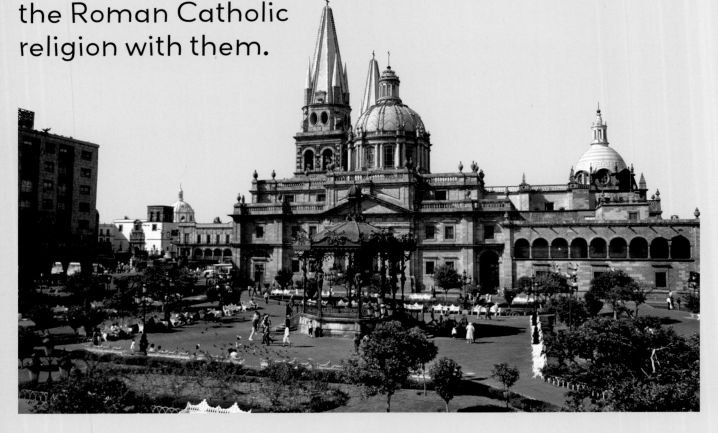

While we are having dinner a group of mariachis walk past playing instruments and singing. Mariachis are musicians who play traditional Mexican music.

The *mariachis* are wearing traditional costumes. They have big, wide sombreros on.

We leave Guadalajara in the morning and go back to Mexico City on the train. From here we are going to fly home. I can't wait to tell all my friends about our trip to Mexico!

My first words in Spanish

Many languages are spoken in Mexico. The most common and official language is Spanish. Mexican Spanish has words from old indigenous languages mixed in too.

Buenos dias
(*say* **Bway-nohs dee-ahs**)   Hello

Adios (*say* **Ah-dee-oss**)   Goodbye

Como estás?
(*say* **Koh-moh ay-stahs**)   How are you?

Como te llamas?
(*say* **Koh-moh tay yah-mahs**)   What is your name?

Me llamo Alice.
(*say* **Mee lah-mo Alice**)   My name is Alice.

Counting 1-10

1 **uno**   2 **dos**   3 **tres**   4 **cuatro**

5 **cinco**   6 **seis**   7 **siete**   8 **ocho**

9 **nueve**   10 **diez**